The 'WHY' Guide Handbook and Reference

Luke Mansfield

Disclaimers

Personal statements or any accusations by the author of criminality or improper conduct by any individual do not serve a purpose and are intentionally avoided by the Y Guide. It is not the case or objective to impose responsibility, blame or criminality on any particular person or group. Y simply wants to relate human behavior to basic human instincts. Likewise, all references to documents, articles, publications, and information are given as information already released to the public by sources in the public eye with established and accepted reputations for providing truthful and valid information. The Y Guide is not responsible for any referenced information that was not properly vetted by the referenced source. Recommended sources are presented for the sole purpose of allowing readers to research and interpret source information. The author has presented information from pertinent sources and subjects with the intention to summarize and paraphrase the content objectively without any intentional bias. It is left to the readers to research and evaluate all researched information and come to their own conclusions. As mentioned, the primary goal is to present information and views that may not be often exposed, especially for the purpose of presenting information to the younger [high school and college age] readers who may not have seen or fully considered such Y ideas and by the same token might stand to benefit more from them.

In researching the Y thesis, the author has drawn and developed inferences, suggestions and conclusions that are solely of his own interpretation, derivation and making. These are not to suggest or infer that any reference, source or content agrees with, suggests, infers, makes or supports the author's or publisher's representations, conclusions or interpretations of researched information.

Acknowledgments

I must acknowledge the sacrifices of my immediate family first and of my siblings, in-laws, and their families. They have always allowed and supported my time given to my solitary pursuits and additionally accepted and 'covered' for me in areas where I may have shirked my duties and not held up my end of the bargain well in terms of my responsibilities, for which I am forever indebted to them.

I must thank the readership for all of the interest and response to the Y Guide. I hope that all find the Y Guide useful, pertinent and a benefit in your daily lives. I hope Y has made the primary point, evidenced and shown that for time immemorial, basic natural human instincts account for man's strongest motivators and behavior that can override other lesser motivations and which can lead to humans' inhumanity and hurtful, aggressive behavior toward fellow humans. The nature of these effects is part of human makeup and a component of the humans' set of inescapable survival and inborn instincts. As humans in society, we may tend to and want to ignore, hide or de-emphasize these traits [we prefer not to contemplate or admit that we can have any innate 'bad' behavior traits or intensions]. However, it is a 'good' thing to recognize and gain perspective so that we may benefit from this realization and knowledge.

I view that my efforts in writing the Y Guide are reflective of my life of not being keenly aware of Y as my life has gone by. With the Y Guide, I am hoping that my observations and conclusions strike a meaningful, truthful and valuable chord that is recognized and shared among my readers. Extending from this experience, more importantly, I am hoping that the Y findings can become available and most valuable to the younger set, particularly in the high school and college-age range, allowing these readers to consider and gain a 'look-ahead' and 'head-start' in understanding human nature, Y, and experiences to come in order to gain the most value, benefit, safety, enjoyment and rewards throughout our lives.

Another point of key importance for me is to dispel any impression that your author is or wants to disparage or cast humans or human nature in a negative or 'bad' light. This might be a pitfall associated with understanding Y and the reason we may want to avoid this subject. However, my view is that, on the contrary, humans are not 'bad' we are just natural and naturally evolved to survive and thrive. To me, humans are the amazing, highest form of life especially owing to our mental capabilities. I love, accept, and admire humans and human nature as-is unequivocally. I want and hope that I am fortunate enough and am thankful to aspire to and be part of the 'mainstream' and 'normal curve' of humans and human nature.

The Y Guide tries to avoid subjects and concepts that do not provide true and worthy evidence, effects and impacts of basic human instincts.

All readers are welcome and invited to provide feedback, analysis, questions, and comments to the published website email address below on any related subject[s]. All subjects are fair game, including politics, behaviors, motivations, social media effects, marketing, entertainment, government, religion, etc. The Email address for readers' feedback is as follows:

marketing@americanpublishersinc.com

Thank you very much, Luke Mansfield.

CONTENTS

Preface and Author Background

My background includes growing up and living my entire life [so far] in one rural location, within a stereotypical lower-middleclass family. I am married with one child. My formal education began with grammar school at a one-room schoolhouse near my home. I am retired from a career as an engineer and developer in the electronics, computer hardware and software design, and electrical power maintenance fields. I have a bachelor's degree in electrical engineering, a master's degree in computer science and had a professional engineering license during my working career.

Out of engineering school, my first job was at a start-up company in my area. At this time, we were experiencing a dramatic transition from vacuum tubes to transistors, integrated circuits and computer technology. I was extremely fortunate to work with and learn from a small group of talented hardware and software engineers and our president who was an entrepreneur, innovator, visionary and leader in these technologies. This group designed, developed and sold some of the first desktop computers. I believe these experiences helped me to appreciate objective observation and to be precise, factual and attentive to detail, and as thorough, unambiguous and concise as possible in designing and documenting the operation of computer equipment. In writing the 'WHY' Guide I feel I have borrowed much from this career and life experience.

Chapter 1: The WHY Guide Introduction

Subject, Objectives, Goals, Credits

The 'WHY' Guide explores and offers an explanation of 'WHY' or the reason[s] we as humans behave as we do and what accounts for basic decisions that we make including human's inhumanity to man as we call it. This 'WHY' is the subject, thesis, and central point of this Guide. 'Y' will be used interchangeably with 'WHY' for convenience.

Y intends to describe and present valid information and references to show that basic human instincts underlie and can predominate our decisions and actions despite our logic and other less powerful considerations. The goals of the Y Guide include the fact that the nature of the motivations involved, since they may not be becoming to our nature, can, therefore, be under-exposed, hidden, or suppressed in our daily lives and discourse.

The Y Guide wants to present the validity and effects of these basic human instincts to all readers but purposefully and especially to younger, developing, and less experienced readers who may gain and benefit the most from the Y thesis and information.

Examples, information and documentation are provided to support the Y thesis, arguments and conclusions. Moreover, 'WHY' is intended as a guide with the purpose of presenting, explaining, understanding, and gaining insight into the basic motivations and reasons for human behavior. As noted, 'WHY,' WHY, 'Y,' and Y are used interchangeably with the same meaning for convenience. The same holds for 'reader,' 'readership,' and 'you,' also for 'author,' 'I,' 'my,' 'your author,' etc.

As mentioned, Y attempts to examine and show why [the strongest reasons] people behave, act, and make decisions that they do. The Y thesis and proposition is that Y is essentially at the most basic and predominant level determined by our basic instincts, which include our basic instincts of survival, self-preservation, self-interest, and self-benefit. The Y Guide develops this thesis and tries to provide undeniable evidence, examples, and information to understand, explain, and substantiate Y. The spectrum of readers is expected to include those who may already agree, believe, and accept the concepts of Y as well as those who may differ or not accept Y at all, but the Y Guide tries to provide enough valid, convincing and true evidence to establish the validity of the Y thesis. The fact that readers can agree or disagree is good and valuable, along with the fact that they are hopefully exposed to the many Y situations that they can evaluate for themselves.

Another espoused benefit of the Y Guide is that, given the basic human instincts that determine human behavior, the reader can explore the information provided but also consider other explanations and reasoning. In addition, understanding, awareness, and consideration of certain behaviors and their causes and consequences can be used to protect, guard against, and avoid threats to our well-being that are consequences of certain Y behaviors.

As noted, the key Y thesis and hypothesis advanced, developed, and evidenced is that humans behave and make decisions based on their inborn natural instincts that can override, predominate, supersede, and displace other motivations and decisions. These instincts include those needed to survive, self-interest, and self-preservation instincts and motivations. One rudimentary but conclusive example of this factor would be the human need and instinct to eat. A human needs to have food to survive and normally instinctively acts to satisfy this basic need. This may seem so obvious that we may not stop to fully appreciate how this instinct must be satisfied. Y tries to show and evidence the effect and overwhelming power of these inborn basic instincts. Y maintains that those basic instincts, including our basic survival instincts, will always be factored predominantly and as needed to the exclusion of other less powerful influences on our decisions to act.

Y does not try to exactly define and enumerate basic and survival instincts, but maintains [the Y thesis] that they unquestionably exist and influence us in an overpowering and predominant way [as the instinctual need for food above]. A key first fact and observation is that the presence and effect of basic instincts are clearly evidenced to have been observable and consistent throughout mankind's existence, throughout the ages, throughout the world, and in all governments, societies, and cultures.

In later chapters, Y will refer to and discuss some of these basic instincts, but more importantly, focus on the fact that they exist and predominate behavior. Y concentrates on the evidence and proof of this type of control over behavior. A study of these behaviors serves to show, if not prove, that these influences exist with dominant power and are part of humans and human nature that we can't deny. Most importantly, by understanding and accepting these behaviors and their derivation, we can at least accept, understand, and protect ourselves with the ultimate goal and fulfillment of being a positive and best model for our fellow humankind and society.

Y wants to help present, show, and understand these types of basic instincts, why they will endure, and that they are 'natural' influences within us. By doing this, we do not need to look away from these characteristics, and additionally, by accepting and understanding them, we can all benefit. This is positive for us and especially the younger developing readers. We want to understand the foundation of these motivations as opposed to taking the incorrect attitude that these traits only exist in 'bad' people. Y takes the position that these are human traits that are 'natural' and affect all of us, so we must learn to deal with them and not ignore that they exist. This is positive and enlightening for us. As we discuss basic instincts and their effects, readers are invited and encouraged to assess, agree, disagree, discuss, and offer their thoughts, discussion, and feedback on instinctive factors that control our decisions.

As the author, I intend to make the Y Guide presentation as simple, uncomplicated, concise, and to the point as possible. To this end, the topics first presented will try to make an unequivocal case supporting Y. Additionally, I will add my personal views and feelings that will allow readers to evaluate and factor my biases, background, and opinions that they may feel contribute properly or improperly to data or conclusions that I represent. I feel this approach prevents and discourages the introduction of many cases, facts, and rhetoric that may unnecessarily cloud the basic thesis. It is hoped that readers will be free to consider, research, comment, and expand on the Y ideas and cases that add dimension to the Y thesis in a valid and useful [positive or negative] way.

Credits and references

The main theme of Y is evidenced and presented as publicly documented examples and substantiated information collected from sources which include the web, Internet, TV programmes, and literature. At this point in history, we have very functional Internet services, with the Internet providing a world-wide physical network infrastructure for accessing, storing, and moving information. The World Wide Web [www] refers to information services, also often referred to as 'Web' services, which also includes 'Wikipedia' as one of the foremost sources of information on a multitude of subjects. Many other well-known services and sites are available, such as Google and YouTube. The author is indebted and grateful for these great resources that are available and so helpful for use by the Y Guide.

The author also accepts that readers and feedback can offer the path, freedom, and opportunity to support or refute any findings or evidence that further augments the information. These web services provide access to vast amounts of information that was previously not practically available or manageable. The author highly recommends the use of these resources and is greatly thankful and appreciative of them. The Y Guide has tried to use and represent these in the most helpful, positive, and best way. I have seen expressions publically that these resources may be lacking in accuracy and corroboration of acts. In any case, I believe we can factor, research, and assimilate such opinions and expressions in a way that helps us to take on more responsibility for corroboration. Additionally and most importantly, the vast amounts of research and data provided by these resources also help us greatly to make valid reflections and judgments on the subject material.

The Y Guide tries to evidence basic instinctive

motivations and cases that drive basic human behavior. In this vein, the most clear and convincing examples, cases, aspects, and arguments are made in order to show that such examples and cases are clear and beyond question. In this regard, many cases that exist are avoided partially for the reason that they might make less than a convincing or unequivocal case of a basic instinctive motivation. This becomes another good case for the welcomed involvement and feedback from readers who can study these examples and apply the Y reasoning to further cases. Along these lines, the reader is invited to study and provide other examples and situations that are attributable to basic instinctual motivations. Feedback and comments sent to the published web and email response sites are encouraged and welcome.

Chapter 2: Prominent Y Examples and Cases

Following are examples from references and documentation that point out and support Y. Rather than attempting to define the basic and survival, deep-routed, inborn instincts and urges that have dominant control of humans' decisions and behaviors, Y first asserts that they exist and have control over actions and decisions. Then, it provides examples that have existed in overwhelming abundance since the beginning of humankind. These behaviors irrefutably prove the existence and the effect of these basic instincts and the resulting Y reasons for these behaviors.

The information below references numerable cases supporting that the problem presented is more basic, instinctual, and common rather than a simple, unusual, unexplained, unique failure in one individual. The examples above show some of the clearest examples of how basic instincts result in many cases of humans behaving in direct contrast to what they espouse and may wish as their purpose and goals in life. Those behaviors, unfortunately, show that many people are more controlled by basic underlying drives and instincts.

Recommended Web Sources and Author Summaries

The information below includes public published information that documents behaviors that the author maintains are the result of Y instincts, motivation, and effects. The author tries to show that this information unequivocally evidences, demonstrates, and validates the Y thesis and premise. Website 'starting/entry point' and Internet 'reference' address information is included with excerpts (author summaries for readers' corroboration) and information to help facilitate independent research, study, corroboration, and evaluation by readers.

2.1 Serial murder cases and references

Below are just a few examples by comparison of the innumerable amount [millions and millions] of murder cases throughout time, the world, and society. As is obvious in our society, life is considered precious, and murder is considered one of the most, if not the most, egregious crimes and legally treated in this regard. The Y thesis is evidenced by the preponderance of these cases, showing that human instinctive motivations can override any and all considerations of the sanctity and value of human life, which is also espoused by humans and supported by societies' norms and laws. Some public information, documentation, and excerpts along with sources are given below.

Recommended Web Sources:

http//en.wikipedia.org/wiki/list_....., 'Wikipedia, list of serial killers by number of victims'.

Author only summary and paraphrasing for readers' corroboration

Reference review: This is a list from throughout the world. The total number of proven victims is 1600 plus. The greatest number of proven victims by one killer is 193; the smallest is 5. 32 killers are listed. In most cases, all of the killers were suspected of killing many more than they were proven of. There were 31 killers listed, all adults [30 men, 1 woman]. There were many cases of sexual crimes against women and children. The woman killer poisoned all of her victims. Note: the above is a very comprehensive, very well-researched article by the source.

Recommended Web Sources:

'Newsweek article
https://www.newsweek,com/most-notable....

Author only summary and paraphrasing for readers' corroboration

Title of article: The Most Notorious Serial Killers in US History and Why

Below are 10 of the most notorious serial killers in US history and the people they killed. Note: below are paraphrased excerpts and information sourced from this article.

Dennis Rader, AKA the BTK Killer

Dennis Rader was a serial killer in Kansas who murdered 10 people over the span of three decades, dubbing himself 'BTK' because he bound, tortured, and killed his victims. He committed his first murders in January of 1974 when he strangled four family members, including two children. He was arrested in 2005 after sending a disk to the police department, which they traced back to the church that Rader served. He confessed to stalking and killings, as well as sexual fantasies that drove his crimes. The BTK Killer received a sentence of 10 consecutive life terms in prison in Kansas.

Ted Bundy

Due to being the subject of several films and documentaries, Ted Bundy is well known for his crimes. Having been described as intelligent and charming, he used his good looks to lure his victims, sexually assaulting and killing at least 36 women across Washington, Oregon, Colorado, Utah, and Florida between 1974 and 1978. Some have estimated he could be responsible for hundreds of deaths. Bundy was ultimately sentenced to death in 1979 for the murder of two college students and again for the rape and murder of a 12-year-old girl. He was executed in Florida by an electric chair in 1989. Note: The names of 26 female victims are identified in the article.

John Wayne Gacy

John Wayne Gacy was responsible for the deaths of at least 33 boys and young men in Chicago in the 1970s, but he has also been used as a figure in the media due to his performance as a party clown at children's parties and social events. He pleaded innocent by reason of insanity, but the jury rejected the psychological evaluations, and Gacy was found guilty of all 33 murders. He was executed via lethal injection in 1994.

Sam Little

Serial killer Samuel Little was known as one of the most prolific killers in American history. Having gone undetected for decades, Little confessed to killing 93 victims in 19 states between 1970 and 2005. According to the FBI, in 2019, law enforcement had been able to verify 50 of the confessions; most of his victims were marginalized, young Black women.

Jeffrey Dahmer

Jeffrey Dahmer, also known as the Milwaukee Cannibal, was a notorious killer and sex offender who killed and dismembered 17 boys and young men between 1978 and 1991. Note: Jeffery Dahmer was murdered in prison in 1994.

Gary Ridgway

Gary Ridgway became known as the Green River Killer and later was known as the deadliest convicted serial killer. He claims to have killed over 80 women in Washington in the 1980s and 90s, but he pled guilty in 2003 to killing 48. In 1980, Ridgway was arrested for choking a prostitute, though no charges were ever filed. He was arrested again for solicitation in 1982, and experts believe his killing spree began shortly after. His first believed victim was said to be a 16-year-old girl whose body was found in the Green River.

Reference Note:

Wikipedia Serial Murderers Documentation

The above document and information from Wikipedia are impressive, detailed, comprehensive, and highly recommended by the author. It represents an extensive amount of research and compilation of data. It reports the names of convicted murderers along with the number of confirmed murders each have committed. It further provides a description of the circumstances and description of the type of murders and offenses committed for each murderer. It additionally reports the additional number of murders that are suspected but not proven for each.

2.2 Clergy

Religious institutions and their supporting clergy must, above all, be acknowledged and recognized for their good work and contributions to mankind and society. Our clergy provide strength, guidance, teaching, and self-sacrifice examples for their following and help sustain and celebrate our belief in a greater power, being, purpose, calling, and meaning of our life on earth.

At the same time, we must also accept the innumerable confirmed cases that contradict the 'life's calling' of some members of our clergy and allow us to question and to deserve, if not require, an explanation of such behavior. Y's place is to provide a valid explanation and reasons for these occurrences. The many cases referenced below demonstrate by example that clergy are human and thus are part of and conform to 'Y'. In this situation, the Y thesis unequivocally explains the most blatant and obvious cases where a human can espouse and present a 'life's calling' while, in truth, hypocritically satisfying a self-serving motivation for themselves. In the same instance, they can hurt many followers and supporters, especially children and young adults. Unfortunately for many victims and society in general, the many cases of abuse by clergy provide very convincing evidence of the Y thesis that basic instincts and motivations exist and will override other more espoused, noble, and honorable presentations.

It is quite a stark example that we see especially in those clergy who present such a unique and espoused dedicated 'life's calling' and then violate this promise by discarding their espoused 'purpose in life' and resorting to only satisfying a more demanding instinct which betrays their espoused faith, hurts and in some cases permanently damages, and ruins others who have trusted and relied on them.

The clergy cases demonstrating Y are widely available, substantiated, and documented. The Y

Guide is definitely not interested in indicting or 'picking on' anyone unfairly, especially clergy. On the contrary, I believe we must also always recognize the many clergy who earn and deserve the highest praise and admiration for their dedication and important role throughout the world and all of the good they and their institutions can and have provided for society. However, at the same time, Y explanations of underlying motivations are fulfilled in these examples of humans' inexcusable violations of espoused purpose, morals, ethics, and trust of followers.

The information below references many cases to show that the problem presented is more basic, primal, instinctual, and common rather than a simple, unusual, unexplained, unique failure in one individual. The examples above show some of the clearest examples of how basic instincts result in many cases of clergy, who are human, behaving in direct contrast to what they espouse is their purpose, objective, and life's dedication and devotion. Those behaviors, unfortunately, may be evidence that there are clergy members who may not have really believed what they are preaching or at least not enough to override their Y instincts and as a result have unfortunately hurt rather than helped their followers. Below are web documentation references and excerpts.

Recommended Web Sources:

[BishopAccountability.org *https://www.bishop-accountability.org/settle...*]

Major Sexual Abuse Settlements in the Catholic Church

Text from the web source: 'In the tables below, we document settlements involving 5,679 persons who allege sexual abuse by Catholic clergy. These survivors are only one-third of the 15,235 allegations that the bishops say they have received.

Recommended Web Sources:

[Article from Albany Times Union Newspaper, ABC News, NBC News [July 2023].

Author only summary and paraphrasing for readers' corroboration

ALBANY — The **Roman Catholic Diocese of Syracuse** has agreed to pay $100 million to hundreds of alleged child sexual abuse victims, marking the second global settlement by a New York diocese and the second-largest contribution by any Catholic institution in a bankruptcy proceeding.

Recommended Web Sources:

[https://www.timesunion.com/state/article/syracuse-diocese-agrees-100m-settle…]

Author only summary and paraphrasing for readers' corroboration

Syracuse diocese agrees to $100M settlement with abuse survivors

Recommended Web Sources:

The Washington Post
https://www.washingtonpost.com/religion/2023/09/29/

Author only summary and paraphrasing for readers' corroboration

Baltimore Catholic archdiocese files for bankruptcy as Clergy

Web: Sep 29, 2023. Baltimore is the 36th US Catholic diocese or religious order to file for such protection since the Catholic clergy sex abuse crisis exploded into public view. The report alleged that more than 600 children were abused in that time frame.

The Catholic Archdiocese of Baltimore filed for bankruptcy protection Friday, less than two days before a new state law takes effect allowing victims of child sexual abuse to sue institutions, no matter how long ago the abuse took place.

Recommended Web Sources:

https://www.catholicnewsagency.com/news/

Author only summary and paraphrasing for readers' corroboration

More Clergy accused of child sexual abuse in California

Web: Dec 2, 2022. By Joe Bukuras. Boston, Mass. As California's three-year window to file child sex abuse lawsuits past the statute of limitations nears its…People also ask: How many clergy abuse lawsuits have led church leaders to bankruptcy?

Over 200 clergy abuse lawsuits led church leaders in the US territory to seek bankruptcy protection, as they estimated at least $45 million in damages.

Recommended Web Sources:

https://www.npr.org/2022/04/20/1093740385

Author only summary and paraphrasing for readers' corroboration

New Jersey Catholic diocese will pay $87.5M to

settle sex ...

Web. Apr 20, 2022. Trenton, NJ. A New Jersey Catholic diocese has agreed to pay $87.5 million to settle claims involving clergy sex abuse with some 300 alleged victims.

2.3 Documentation and Cases Provided by TV Crime Shows and Productions

Hats off to TV crime shows that now seem to be very popular, available in increasing numbers, and appearing on multiple networks and stations. These shows document and present crime cases, which allow us to see Y motivations and behaviors. Historically, some of the original shows of this genre included *Unsolved Mysteries With Robert Stack* began in 1987. This and other forerunner TV shows are referenced below. The classical historical model for the modern shows is *'Forensic Files,'* which began in 1996 and is still popular and rerun today.

The typical presentation for this show and many others now available includes a) a description and re-enactment of a crime, b) the documentation and story of the investigation and evidence, c) a presentation and result of the solution to the crime [usually involving a court case result, perpetrators, names, sentences, etc.]. Most importantly, from the Y standpoint, these cases involve evidence of the human instincts of antisocial and inhumane Y behavior toward other humans, which typically involve murder, rape, and violence.

Another Y aspect would appear to be that these shows and crime stories attract viewers, possibly because they present the basic instinctual motivations and behaviors, and because of this, they draw and captivate viewers who can, in this way, observe and study these basic Y instincts. Below are partial lists of the many crime TV networks and shows. The number of networks and shows is continuously expanding and proliferating due to the popularity of these shows. Readers are encouraged to view these shows for entertainment and to study and understand the Y motivations presented.

Networks

HLN [Headline News, subsidiary of CNN network]; ID [Investigation Discovery, a subsidiary of Warner Bros Discovery network]; NBC [National Broadcasting Company] and Oxygen True Crime [subsidiaries of NBC Universal Media Group]; CBS

[Columbia Broadcasting System], plus others.

TV shows [titles]

Dateline; Secrets Uncovered, Unforgettable [und other titles], Snapped, Dateline Secrets Uncovered, Dateline Unforgettable, 20/20, Deadline: Crime with Tamron Hall, On the case with Paula Zahn, American Detective with Lt. Joe Kenda, Dateline and 48 hours, Real Time Crime begun 2023, Snapped, Dateline Secrets Uncovered, Dateline Unforgettable, Dateline Secrets Uncovered, Dateline Unforgettable, True crime, takedown with Chris Hansen

Crime show development history [honorable mention]

There are a number of TV crime shows that deserve mention because they brought the genre and study of crime to light in TV format and helped to popularize and inspire the many TV productions that are now available and widely viewed. Some of these are listed below.

Cops TV show, began 1989 [Fox Network]: this is one TV show, among other shows, that has a long standing and popularity. It shows live interactions of on-duty police officers in their on-the-job daily activities. America's Most Wanted, began 1988 [Fox

TV network]. Host John Walsh was already well known because of the murder of his son and his subsequent actions to help missing and exploited children. Unsolved Mysteries, hosted by Robert Stack, began 1987. This TV show included presentations and studies of cold crime cases, other topics, and unresolved phenomena.

Crime TV show anecdote:

As an example of many crime shows your author and his family have viewed, I would like to point out, congratulate, and give praise to 'Dateline' for a particular episode below. It exemplifies a very well-researched and produced documentary and organized presentation of a very complicated and multifaceted story. I highly recommend viewing this episode, although it must be said there are many like TV productions on this theme that are extremely well done, entertaining, and enlightening. This one is a 2024 Dateline NBC production hosted by one of their well-established hosts. The title was *'True Confession.'* There were many story twists, turns, and drama. In my view, the plot, intricacies, human tragedy, suffering, and complications could provide the most rich and fascinating movie – not to mention that it is a true story and involves Y. Below is a highly summarized outline of the story.

Summary of the [true] story

A single, upstanding girl in her late teens living in Idaho Falls was raped and brutally murdered. The TV presentation shows a summary of the case and how it was solved. The story shows how a suspect was erroneously suspected, arrested, interrogated, tried, and convicted. Years later, errors were found by authorities, which led to legal redress that reversed the decision after the real perpetrator was found and convicted. The mother of the victim was absolutely essential and gets the most credit for pursuing the case for decades leading to the successful solution [a story in itself].

The most complex conditions, steps, and expertise that led to [a historical forerunner DNA case] isolation of the perpetrator is another whole story in itself. The perpetrator went free and undetected for over 25 years but confessed to the full crime and details once confronted with the DNA proof. The innocent but originally convicted person, who spent years in prison until the case was resolved, suffered a regrettably tragic existence and death [another story in itself].

Author's comments: Y aspects within this story

27

This and countless other cases share and reveal, in the author's view, basic, essential, indisputable Y motivations. The perpetrator above demonstrated that his desire and motivation for his own sexual pleasure and satisfaction also included his total disregard for the well-being of the victim [or anyone but himself]. The fact that he carried on a normal family life and existence for some 30 years before being found-out shows his continued essential instinct for self-preservation and avoidance of any pain, punishment, or concern, let alone consequences, for the people he directly caused harm to. He instinctively chose, without remorse or regret, to avoid any pain or punishment detrimental to himself and his well-being until he was found out through a DNA technology-related investigation. This is a powerful story and example of Y.

2.4 Cults

Cults are a subject of key interest and relevance directly related to Y motivations, instincts, and behaviors. Some information and cases from Web searches are given below.

Definitions

Merriam Webster Web source 'a religion regarded as unorthodox or spurious.' Oxford Dictionary Web source 'a relatively small group of people having beliefs or practices, especially relating to religion, that are regarded by others as strange or sinister or as imposing excessive control over members.'

Recommended Web Sources:

https://www.psychologytoday.com/us/blog/freedom-mind/202106/understanding-cults-.....

Author only summary and paraphrasing for readers' corroboration

Title: Understanding Cults – The Basics [from 'Psychology Today' site]

- Cults use deception and undue influence to make people dependent and obedient.
- Cults are typically authoritarian, headed by a person or group of people with near complete control of followers.
- Cults are attractive because they promote an illusion of comfort.
- Cults satisfy the human desire for absolute answers.
- Those with low self-esteem are more likely to be persuaded by a cult environment.
- Understanding cults involves recognizing the following key points:

- A cult is an organized group that uses psychological manipulation and pressure strategies to dominate its members.
- Cults are often led by a powerful leader who isolates members from society.
- Cult influence disrupts a person's authentic identity and replaces it with a new one.
- Cults can take various forms, including religious, political, self-help, or online groups.
- The basics to help others; it is important to understand mind control and undue influence.
- No one joins a cult; they are recruited by systematic social influence processes.
- Destructive individuals and cults use deception and undue influence to make people dependent and obedient.
- Not all influence is bad. There is a difference between due and undue influence.
- Cult leaders are typically malignant narcissists and want people who will be obedient to them.

Recommended Web Sources:

https://www....5 Most Ruthlessly Infamous Cult Leaders In History | Stillunfold......

Author only summary and paraphrasing for readers' corroboration

Title: 5 Most Ruthlessly Infamous Cult Leaders in History

Jim Jones

James Warren Jones, or Jim Jones (as he was popularly known), was an American cult leader who founded the religious cult 'Peoples Temple' in the 1950s. Jones was influenced by communism and was appointed as a priest of the Disciples of Christ. After moving the cult to California in the 1960s, he gained infamy as the cult leader for the violent activities carried out in San Francisco in the 1970s.

In 1978, there were media reports about the human rights violations and prevailing abuses that were happening in the People's Temple Jonestown, located in Guyana. While probing into the matter, Leo Ryan was shot to death as he boarded a return flight with traitors.

A few hours after his murder, the mass murder-suicide of his 918 followers took place in Jonestown, Guyana. Around 300 children were murdered, most of them were poisoned by Flavor Aid mixed with cyanide poison. This historical event, dubbed as 'revolutionary suicide,' led to the coinage of the ubiquitous American-English expression 'drinking the Kool-Aid.'

Shoko Asahara

Shoko Asahara, the founder of the Japanese doomsday cult group 'Aum Shinrikyo,' was the mastermind responsible for the 1995 Sarin gas attack on the Tokyo subway. Asahara was convicted of the said attack and many other crimes. In 2004, he was sentenced to death. Asahara's execution was postponed in June 2012 because of further arrests of his cult members.

Charles Milles Manson (born Charles Milles Maddox)

Charles Milles Manson, or simply Charles Manson, is an American criminal and former cult leader of the quasi-commune Manson Family that emerged in California during the 1960s. In July-August 1967, Manson's followers committed 9 murders in a row at 4 locations.

In 1971, Manson was convicted of first-degree murder and conspiracy to murder 7 people (most notably actress Sharon Tate) that were carried by cult members at Manson's direction. Currently, he is serving lifetime imprisonment at the California State

Prison in Corcoran.

David Koresh (born Vernon Wayne Howell)

David Koresh was the American cult leader of Branch Davidians who originated around 1955 and believed himself to be its final prophet. Koresh was later condemned for statutory rape of a 12-year-old girl, a relationship that he sanctified as a 'spiritual marriage.'

The 1993 historic raid caused ATF's probe into illegal possession of firearms and explosives. During the early 2-hour firefight, 4 ATF agents and 6 Davidians were killed. The following siege by the FBI ended with a conflagration in which Koresh and 79 others were found dead.

Marshall Herff Applewhite, Jr. (aka 'Bo' and 'Do')

Marshall Applewhite was an American cult leader who founded the UFO religious millenarian group 'Heaven's Gate' and carried out mass suicides in 1997 that claimed 39 lives.

Sex Cults

Below is an outline example of the many sex cults. This example comes from Wikipedia, which provides comprehensive reporting, documentation, and detail.

Author only summary and paraphrasing for readers' corroboration

Title: [from the Wikipedia free encyclopedia] 'NXIVM'

NXIVM was a cult led by convicted racketeer and sex offender Keith Raniere. NXIVM is also the name of the defunct company that Raniere founded in 1998, which provided seminars ostensibly about human potential development and served as a front organization for criminal activity by Raniere and his close associates.[3][5] Following Raniere's conviction in 2019, the Department of Justice seized ownership of NXIVM-related entities and their intellectual property through asset forfeiture.

Author Closing Comments on Cults and Y Relevance

The above information evidences Y instincts, motivations and behaviors. Cult leaders clearly evidence and demonstrate profound Y basic instincts, which include humans' desire to use, benefit, and manipulate others to gain support, benefits, and sustenance for themselves without any necessary consideration or obligation to meaningfully benefit others.

Chapter 3: Author Personal Views & Observations

Below are some of my personal views and opinions on subjects involving Y. These are separated from earlier information that contains only sourced references and facts to support Y fully on their own merit. In contrast, this chapter contains factual information and sources but includes my own perspectives, opinions [and any biases?] that I may have, but which try to show Y motives and behaviors. Rather than attempting to impose or enforce my own opinions on readers anyone, my most important objective is to offer, welcome, and invite the readership to review, consider, and give feedback to assess the author's biases and perspectives and then to agree or disagree.

These represent a full career through retirement and a few decades of work in creating the Y guide. The credence and value that I see of these views will be measured by what the readership assigns from your consideration, acceptance, and feedback. This response will shape my views and allow me to see and understand how my views are supportable or not, accurate or inaccurate, based on a comparison with a consensus and feedback from readers.

As the views below contain my personal

perceptions along with factual information, I am hoping the readers' feedback will enhance my perspective.

Relevant Books Recommended

Civilization and its Discontents, Sigmund Freud, 1930

This is a renowned book that is recommended and, among all works, might be the one that most directly connects with the Y Guide theme as it gives Freud's explanation, understanding, and analysis of the basic components of human nature and psychology at the root of human's essence in terms of thought, instincts, and behavior. I think it's ideas are profound and relate to Y in that Freud had a life and profession immersed in these thoughts, ideas, and research as a psychotherapist. I believe Y supports Freud's work by evidencing behaviors and reasons [basic instincts and survival behaviors] that are unchangeable and essential for humans' existence. Web articles detail the ideas presented in the book in which Freud describes how immutable, inborn, deep-seated instincts and desires of humans are in conflict, tension, and opposition [discontents] to the desires, goals, and objectives of civilized societies.

Key Words and Personality Definitions in Freud's

Book & Theory

Recommended Web Sources:

https://wikipedia.org/wiki/id...<u>Id, ego and superego - Wikipedia</u>

Author only summary and paraphrasing for Readers' corroboration

'Ego'

The ego acts according to the reality principle. Since the id's drives are frequently incompatible with social reality, the ego attempts to direct its energy and satisfy its demands in accordance with the imperatives of that reality. According to Freud, the ego, in its role as mediator between the id and reality, is often 'obliged to cloak the (unconscious) commands of the id with its own preconscious rationalizations, to conceal the id's conflicts with reality, to profess...to be taking notice of reality even when the id has remained rigid and unyielding.'

Originally, Freud used the word ego to mean the sense of self but later expanded it to include psychic functions such as judgment, tolerance, reality testing, control, planning, defense, synthesis of information, intellectual functioning, and memory. The ego is the organizing principle upon which thoughts and interpretations of the world are based.

According to Freud, 'the ego is that part of the id which has been modified by the direct influence of the external world....The ego represents what may be called reason and common sense, in contrast to the id, which contains the passions...it is like a tug of war...with the difference that in the tug of war the teams fight against one another in equality, while the ego is against the much stronger 'id.' In fact, the ego is required to serve 'three severe masters...the external world, the superego, and the id. It seeks to find a balance between the primitive drives of the id, the limitations imposed by reality, and the structures of the superego. It is concerned with self-preservation: it strives to keep the id's desires within limits, adapted to reality and submissive to the superego.

'Superego'

The superego reflects the internalization of cultural rules, mainly as absorbed from parents, but also other authority figures, and the general cultural ethos. Freud developed his concept of the superego from an earlier combination of the ego ideal and the 'special psychical agency which performs the task of seeing that narcissistic satisfaction from the ego ideal is ensured...what we call our 'conscience.' For him, the superego can be described as 'a successful instance of identification with the parental agency,' and as development proceeds it also absorbs the influence of those who have 'stepped into the place of parents—educators, teachers, people chosen as ideal models.'

Thus, a child's superego is, in fact, constructed on the model not of its parents but of its parents' superego; the contents that fill it are the same, and it becomes the vehicle of tradition and of all the time-resisting judgments of value which have propagated themselves in this manner from generation to generation.

The superego aims for perfection. It is the part of the personality structure, mainly but not entirely unconscious, that includes the individual's ego ideals, spiritual goals, and the psychic agency, commonly called 'conscience,' that criticizes and prohibits the expression of drives, fantasies, feelings, and actions. Thus, the superego works in contradiction to the id. It is an internalized mechanism that operates to confine the ego to socially acceptable behavior, whereas the id merely seeks instant self-gratification.

The superego and the ego are the product of two key factors: the state of helplessness of the child and the Oedipus complex. In the case of the little boy, it forms during the dissolution of the Oedipus complex through a process of identification with the father figure following the failure to retain possession of the mother as a love-object out of fear of castration. Freud described the superego and its relationship to the father figure and the Oedipus complex thus: the superego retains the character of the father, while the more powerful [the Oedipus complex] was and the more rapidly it succumbed to repression (under the influence of authority, religious teaching, schooling and reading), the stricter the domination of the superego over the ego later on—in the form of conscience or perhaps of an unconscious sense of guilt.

'Id'

Freud conceived the id as the unconscious source of bodily needs and wants, emotional impulses and desires, especially aggression and the sexual drive. The id acts according to the 'pleasure principle'—the psychic force oriented to the immediate gratification of impulse and desire.

Freud described the id as 'the dark, inaccessible part of our personality.' Understanding of the id is limited to the analysis of dreams and neurotic

41

symptoms, and it can only be described in terms of its contrast with the ego. It has no organization and no collective will: it is concerned only with the satisfaction of drives in accordance with the pleasure principle. It is oblivious to reason and the presumptions of ordinary conscious life: 'contrary impulses exist side by side, without cancelling each other....There is nothing in the id that could be compared with negation...nothing in the id which corresponds to the idea of time. The id 'knows no judgments of value: no good and evil, no morality.

Developmentally, the id precedes the ego. The id consists of the basic instinctual drives that are present at birth, inherent in the somatic organization, and governed only by the pleasure principle. The psychic apparatus begins as an undifferentiated id, part of which then develops into a structured 'ego,' a concept of self that takes the principle of reality into account.

Author reflections

An important theme of Freud's work, in my view, is that civilization presents standards, demands, and resulting conflicts between society and humans. Also, it is most interesting to me that the ideas in Freud's book very directly relate to and coincide with Y. Freud identifies and describes the basic drives that humans respond to. I feel that Y augments Freud's work by providing substantiating evidence and examples where the results of these drives have been actualized and documented. Freud's book is highly recommended reading. It seems to me consistent with Freud's theories that Y motivations, decisions and behavior might be considered cases of the 'ID' actualization and dominance over the 'EGO.' It may be worth noting that Freud's theory as such did not use or need to site documented examples as proof. However, in today's world, given the great web resources and social media services, the Y guide is able to provide cases to further support Freud's analyses and work.

I feel that I have no standing or credentials that compare in any measure to those of Sigmund Freud, who spent his life's dedication and career to achieve the experience, expertise, and knowledge that he represented and advanced in his ground-breaking book and his life's profession in the psychology-related fields.

My positive view is that Y examples and documentation are consistent with and supportive of Freud. Compared with the era of Freud and his work, the vast web resources available now also allow us to study and augment Freud's theories and work. This is a luxury and opportunity for us now that was not available for Freud.

The Origin of Species by Charles Darwin, 1859

This book is an astoundingly, immense, in-depth, detailed, and comprehensive study of evolution and how all of life has developed and adapted through all of time. It is such an amazing undertaking in its amount of research, application of the scientific principle, time, and effort. It is highly recommended for all of its above qualities. Of course, Y is directly related in that it agrees and supports the idea that human life, exactly as Darwin covers for all life, is inextricably tied to and dependent upon basic essential instincts and survival abilities that have developed and evolved over the duration of life and which are only subject to evolutionary adaptive change as necessary over extended periods. Again, the scientific findings, conclusions, and accomplishments of Darwin are astounding. It is interesting to note that in spite of his extensive, dramatic efforts and scientific achievements, Darwin was notably and strongly rebuked and attacked by clergy, who took his extensive scientific proof and evidence of evolution as an assault on creationism. This aspect is expanded in web and Wikipedia documentation.

Words and language [words are terrible things?]

As we know, words provide our primary and most basic and essential way of expression and communication with other humans. This communication ability encompasses all aspects of our lives: wants, desires, feelings, opinions, etc. There are many languages around the world that fulfill this need and purpose. As babies and youngsters, language is one the first things we are exposed to and which we intellectually 'pick-up' and utilize. Starting in school we formally enhance and expand on this knowledge and word usage.

The reader is invited to explore and develop further examples but suffice it to say words and human nature have parallels and analogies. For many years prior to working on the Y Guide, I had espoused 'words are terrible things.' This was because I had concluded that many unsolvable interpretations and misinterpretations would make motivations, meaning, and intent imprecise and concealed. Among literature and books, I concluded that only science and math-type textbooks provided unambiguous, precise and 'to-the-point' meaning. Although I now accept words as necessary for better or worse, the use and function of words and language have added to my development, genesis, and path to Y.

Antisocial words and assignment problems

There are many words used to describe antisocial activity and thoughts. I will use 'narcissism' as a typical example to illustrate a common point about such personality aspects. The point is that any of these personality assignments represent a spectrum or range. For instance, narcissism is defined as: selfishness, involving a sense of entitlement, a lack of empathy, and a need for admiration, as characterizing a personality type [Oxford Language Dictionary].

In the author's view, to describe a person as narcissistic is more condemning and assaulting than accurate and fair and too imprecise because this label does not distinguish where on the spectrum a 'narcissist' might be. To go one step further, I feel that these and all personality traits worth examination are shared to some degree by all, including all 'normal' people. I believe that we all clearly have some degree of narcissism, ego, hate, and 'bad' behavior or psychological negatives to some degree. Therefore, it is not useful to call someone narcissistic without further delineating their position within the spectrum. Without this placement in the spectrum, I feel the narcissism label is more unfairly punitive than helpful.

Why do we laugh? What is humor?

Why do jokes and humor make us laugh and why do we find things 'funny?' Y believes that 'laughing' is a basic aspect and instinct of human nature. It seems that virtually all normal humans can and do laugh, which further relates this behavior to basic 'Y' instincts. We know that this human characteristic is shared throughout human nature, the world, and human history. It is also the case that 'laughing' as we know it is not seen in other animals, thus relating it to humans' exceptional and unique mental capabilities among animals. This response is also spontaneous without pre-consideration or even pre-thought.

At a more foundational level, Y views laughter as a very basic instinctual response related to unrestricted exhilaration and celebration in response to some key situations, including: a) 'winning' or 'superiority' in games, sports and human completion, b) the realization that we have overcome or vanquished and eliminated any possible threat or danger and have proven our superiority and unquestionable dominance over another human or human situation. We will spontaneously laugh and celebrate this feeling as a basic human instinct. To 'make fun' of someone or something involving humans gets us closer to the Y instincts of survival and success that we need and depend on. Humor and jokes involve a situation that casts another human [the subject or brunt of the joke] as incompetent, incapable, or foolish and thus creates the feeling of 'winning' and superiority over the subject—this makes us happy and proves our survivability.

When researched on the Web, 'funny' equates to 'pleasurable, relaxing, enjoyable.' Moreover, Y views that spontaneous laughing at humor and jokes involves receiving the instinctual 'signal' that we can 'win' and dominate others for our own survival and benefit, which immediately excites us and makes us 'happy.' As noted, this kind of happiness, smiling, laughter, and celebration also occurs when our favorite sports team or contestant wins [discussed later], and in contrast, the losing side does not smile or laugh. Related smiling can be a precursor and on the path to laughing.

Self-deprecating humor - Definition from Web and Y explanation

This information from the web provides insight and support of the Y explanation of humor and why we laugh that is not typically presented. As it describes, this humor is pointing out a weakness in ourselves. Y sees this as consistent with the reasoning that if one observes someone else as weak or incompetent, then the observer 'wins' and will laugh for this reason. Seeing that he is an unchallenged 'winner,' he will immediately celebrate this with a laugh or smile.

The 'presentation' laugh

The Y laugh is an uncalculated, unplanned, unpredicted result of a basic instinctual motivation, as described earlier. It is a spontaneous and instantaneous reaction to an external input, stimulus, or idea. There is another type of laugh or smile that we will call 'manufactured', 'presented,' or 'calculated' because it has a totally distinct origin and cause. This manufactured laugh, unlike the spontaneous Y laugh, is totally planned and 'presented' for some calculated effect. We all seem to be able to produce or create and 'calculate' a smile or laugh to create the impression that we are successful and happy [and a 'winner']. We see this in our photographs, advertisements, movies, etc. Again, the key distinction is that a Y laugh is spontaneous, unplanned, and uncalculated, whereas a 'presentation' laugh has a different origin as described.

Babies laughter

Y views that this basic instinctive motivation also, naturally, is present in babies. Here, we can see that babies often laugh after being tickled, surprised, or startled. Y views that, in this case, 1) this is a basic instinct, and 2) Y sees laughing from babies like adults as a basic instinctive response. When babies are startled, surprised, or frightened and recover after knowing that no harm has come to them, they respond by laughing—an expression of relief, celebration, and happiness that 'they are ok' and thus have enjoyed the experience, which was exciting and not harmful. Likewise, tickling can lead to a baby's laughter, and again, this is attributed to a surprise, startling effect on the baby, after which the baby will recover, laugh, and be happy as a result of a friendly, reassuring connection from those it is with. This reasoning is covered in further depth in web articles.

Why do babies cry

For babies, crying is an aspect of key importance in their infant lives. Interestingly and naturally in all of the billions of cases, we know babies cannot explain why they are crying. But in terms of Y, babies are dependent on adult care and very incapable of providing some of their own essential needs [example:

food]. A basic Y instinct and self-preservation for the baby is to express a need by crying. The need may arise from hunger, pain, discomfort, etc. The baby cries, the caregiver gets this signal and normally will be able to determine and satisfy the need [resolve the baby's problem], and then the baby will stop crying.

Winning and losing, competition, games, sports, contests

It is interesting that a human sports event, first of all, results in competition and a winner and loser. This is human—we get interested and exited because this aspect is confirmation of success and our success as a spectator if we favor the winner. It solidifies prosperity and the ability to survive against impediments and other humans. Along these lines it is interesting that the winning side of these sports events is full of smiles and laughter while the losers are 'down,' frustrated and unhappy. This is the case even though the difference between winning and losing might only be the tiniest difference in scores, and beyond this, it has no other benefit for the spectator beyond 'happiness' from 'beating' the opponent [we have overcome and vanquished the threat working against us]. These sports and contests at least provide us with a type of contest and competition that best avoids violent confrontations in determining who dominates.

My sexual development comments

This progression and development may fill a book for each of us, but here is a brief overview of my experiences and feelings. I believe my sexual development was within the normal curve as a male. At puberty and into adolescence, I began to be physically and sexually attracted to females, especially my age group. I believe in my case, and for normal instinctual reasons, I began to be attracted and gravitate to the females around me. Their characteristics [visual appearance, personality, names, and other characteristics] formed my standard of comparison and, from that point, what I looked for in other females and who I was most attracted to. I think this most critical development stage of life was based not on logic or intellect [not figured out or calculated], but rather on my basic instinctual effects: appearance, personality, sensory inputs, and feelings during this stage. At puberty and adolescence, I started to be noticeably attracted to the females of my age around me. Notably, I formed what became my models of attraction from these females, who became models throughout my life for their physical and personality attributes.

Female vs. male Y sexual instincts in the prime of life

Pre-puberty is an important study but Y feels that behaviors at these earlier stages do not have as great an effect on actions during this phase and age. Likewise, puberty and adolescence are of key importance, but the ramifications again become more important and influential in adulthood as we settle into our acceptable behaviors as adult males and females in our prime [from post-adolescence/puberty till post-childbearing ages]. Pre-puberty is an important study, but Y feels that behaviors at these earlier stages do not have as great an effect at this age, and decisions and effects are not as directly important. Likewise, the ramifications of adolescence and puberty again become more significant in adulthood.

Females

For females, the instincts seem to be more diverse. Females in their prime, unlike men, have a strong instinct for motherhood, rearing and raising children. From the author's point of view, females, moreover, have a more diverse set of standards, goals, and objectives that they look to fulfill. Underneath the above primary motivators are many others that affect their behaviors. But to reemphasis the motherhood instinct is primary in females vs. the fatherhood instinct in males.

Males

Of course, there are many instincts that motivate male behavior, but statistically, the outstanding dominating instinct of the majority of normal men in their prime seems to be satisfying their sexual objectives.

Supportive Y examples, strip clubs, prostitution

Some differences in basic instincts between men and women in the normal curve explain Y there are 'strip clubs' throughout the country [and world?] where females expose their bodies to audiences of excited, interested, 'paying' males. This is telling as strip clubs in which males strip for females are comparatively non-existent [and ludicrous?], i.e., males are much more interested and motivated [as a sexual instinct] in the female nude body than are females in the male nude body by comparison. It is accepted that many other behaviors arise from this basic instinctual motivation.

Prostitution is widely referred to as 'the world's oldest profession.' It stands out as a very simple, perfect, basic, and representative example and proof of the Y thesis. Moreover, from the Y standpoint, prostitution has existed throughout time and all humanity as a proven, evidenced basic human instinct. Interestingly, we can further see clearly how these instincts distinguish females from males, i.e., females and males fulfill unique roles in classic prostitution as we know. Typically within the mainstream and normal curve, the male engages in prostitution by providing material benefits to the female in exchange for sexual pleasure that the female provides. Typically, the female commensurately provides sexual pleasure to the male in exchange for material benefits received. Classically, the reverse roles do not come into play. The roles are specifically very different and expose the basic instincts and motivations between males and females, which are unique and unmistakable and serve to further explain other behaviors that differentiate the sexes.

Bragging and Y

'Boasting,' 'self-aggrandizement,' and 'touting' are words with similar meanings. It would seem that we all individually have a scale and an arbitrary 'line' above which a person representing his talents, abilities, accomplishments, worth, etc., is considered to be 'bragging.' Looking at the Y perspective I think it must be understood that we all must be able to recognize and have the ability for 'self-accomplishment.' Thus, even if we are not viewed as 'braggers,' we still have to recognize and accomplish tasks and goals for our own well-being and satisfaction. This is why the seeds and foundations of bragging are instinctive and a Y component of human nature. So, at a basic level, we can say that we are all 'braggers.' Moreover, the author views 'bragging' as a Y human instinct that relates to the human need to 1) achieve basic survival requirements and accomplishments and 2) promote these successes and feel good about them.

When we succeed, it is obviously rewarding, and we must accept and must use these successes as contributing to our well-being and must use the confidence achieved to build on them and pursue other needed accomplishments. How we view excessive 'bragging' is a personal judgment that varies and we should be aware that we all have to brag [at least to ourselves] as a way to continue to find success for ourselves. Thus, in conclusion, we are all involved in [the instinct of] bragging to some degree as part of survival and 'Y.' As with other assessments and terms describing human behavior, bragging is a behavior on a 'spectrum.' We can each assess some bragging as either 'over the line' or 'acceptable.' We also must see and accept a certain level of bragging in everyone for the same reason.

One example of this is clearly expressed and presented in commercial advertising. The basic presentation of advertisers is to present that their service or product is 'better' and 'superior' to the competition. This is bragging, but it also expresses qualities and success that we are attracted to, qualities we like and which help us and thus are considered good, so we tend not to associate it with bragging!

Religion

I was baptized and attended church as a child but drifted away from the church in later years. There is a well-documented history of many religions, religious beliefs, and worship of a 'Higher being,' 'meaning of life,' and 'Gods' throughout time. I would suggest this aspect is a basic instinct of humankind— relating to the desire to understand the origin and most basic purpose of man, life, and the universe. This view is taken because religious behaviors seem widely variable depending on the era in which they have been observed and followed. My feeling is that religions, among other things, have survived to provide us with a reason and answer to explain our existence, how we and the universe were created, and why we are here—this becomes a higher intellectual inquiry that we as humans want to have an answer for.

My feeling about religion tends toward what I feel exists among many scientifically oriented people. Those of a scientific background and orientation seem to reach a dead end as religious doctrine seems to reach further and seems to try, unsuccessfully, to explain everything. The answers seem to come up short for me as well. However, I believe that religion can be a needed and good force in a very basic way for humanity. This, to me, can be expressed in a simple message of the golden rule; 'treat others as you would have others treat you' and be kind and respectful to others under all circumstances. This view allows me to avoid a deeper study, worship practices, time spent, commitment to doctrine and other special religious practices. It also allows me to avoid the debate involving assertions and feelings of those who seem to blame and use 'religion' as a cause or reason for dissension between religions and religious beliefs.

'Understanding is acceptance'

You may have heard the phrase 'understanding is acceptance.' I believe this statement has validity. For example, take the case of violence such as murder as a consequence and expression of hate. I believe that the seeds of hate extending to violence is a motivation force. To me, these seeds of hate and examples of violence extending from hate involve basic instincts within all humans and human nature. When violence such as murder is committed, our laws come into effect that dictate how this 'crime' is acknowledged and treated as 'unacceptable' for our society.

However, it remains that these offenses occur in all parts of society and have occurred since the beginning of time. Based on a view and recognition of 'hate,' I see and accept this underlying motivation and behavior as something 'normal' and existing as a motivator in normal humans. I further believe that when we don't accept these motivators as normal human nature, it causes us to 'hide' these motivators as if they are so horrible that they don't exist in normal human behavior. My view is that by understanding and, in so doing, accepting these motivators as normal rather than hiding them, we can study these behaviors and benefit by using our enlightenment and intelligence to further prevent and avoid these 'bad' behaviors in society.

Social media influences

The new generation of technology providing

social media access and communications between us seems to have noticeable effects. From a Y standpoint, this makes sense. Basic instincts are to be relevant, to be able to establish a forum for our views, and to achieve confirmation that our views and opinions are worthwhile and valid, if not absolutely correct. Through social media, we are able to present our views and ideas to many. For good and bad, we can also do this quite anonymously which adds to our freedom and avoidance of 'push back' and offensive repercussions. Additionally, the fact that we can be exposed to and consider so many more opinions and views provided by social media allows us to see a wider range of views. It also allows us to assimilate a diversity of views and hold any particular view especially by an 'authority' less substantial and carrying less weight. The result of these seems to be more dissension, disagreement, diversity, and non-conformity, which seems to make sense. As a result, this seems to expose and accentuate our differences and is evidenced by more dissension in our society as opposed to more uniformity of our attitudes, standards, and views. These effects and exposure, positive and negative, seem to also attribute and increase in questions and distrust of our government leadership and institutions. I am interested in receiving more views and feedback on this view.

US culture, government, institutions, capitalism, politics

As a US citizen, my political preferences are 'Independent' and 'Libertarian.' I am a supporter of our US political system because it underlies a long-lasting, safe, and high standard of living for us in the US among world countries and areas. I believe our founders provided for our economic success, freedom, and independence in comparison with other countries of the world. I believe our democratic freedoms, work ethic, capitalism, and military institutions have helped our overall success for ourselves and the world. I believe our educational institutions have provided a great benefit for us and our country. Our education provides the foundation for us to evaluate and make our best and most informed life choices in virtually all aspects of our lives [vocational career, leisure, government, products, services, etc.].

As with any civilization, I think that we are not perfect and have made serious mistakes, but I believe our political system has allowed us to incrementally, safely and positively correct mistakes and 'wrongs' to make progress and improvements while maintaining our strengths and positive attributes. I also believe that our systems and culture support and incorporate certain Y realities that are an overall positive for our society.

Abortion: laws, politics, and views

This topic has prominently presented itself to our society and government. It is only included in the Y Guide because this topic parallels the feelings and complexity of humans, human nature, and Y issues. Medical science and advancements have provided for abortions and related health benefits, but now we are faced with problems that beg for a political resolution. Some of the problems include the following:

- Some who believe in the absolute sanctity and protection of life will not accept abortion at all.

- Some believe that health concerns for the mother should allow some abortions.

- Some believe in a time restriction that allows abortion only after a minimum period after conception.

- Some believe that abortion should be allowed at any time.

- Some believe that abortion should only be

decided by the mother and her doctor.

- Constitutionally, the federal government has relinquished legal control of the issue to the states.

There does not seem to yet be an acceptable, workable, practical agreement between all government authorities. The degree of dissension on acceptance and policy within our greater population, in my view, suggests that this will remain an issue in our society without full resolution for some time to come.

Ending Comments

Within this chapter of personal views, the intent has been to distinctly separate my personal views related to Y from the initial chapters, which provide 'stand-alone' documented evidence of Y. I want to re-iterate my interest in readers to provide feedback and email comments, which will add perspective for all of us.

Chapter 4: Y Guide Closing Comments

The purpose of the Y Guide has been to evidence and present in a concise way that our [human] decisions and behaviors are inescapably and at a basic level overridingly controlled by our own most basic, inborn, deep-seated, and strongest instincts for better or for worse. The main interest and objectives have been to concisely and convincingly present cases and evidence that demonstrate and show that humans' strongest motivations and behaviors are a result of basic inherent instincts that do not change and have been present throughout time and humanity. Further, in view of humans' inhumanity to humans, these motivations can be left under-exposed or ignored, which, therefore, unfortunately, do not become a life lesson that could help inexperienced and younger people avoid negative impacts related to Y.

Presentation of these ideas and evidence in the initial chapters is followed by some subjective views of the author in chapter 3. It is hoped that those subjective views will promote and encourage independent thought, study, consideration and research of those viewpoints which will promote your own conclusions supporting or contrasting with mine. Your feedback and discussion of Y ideas will also expand my views, education and knowledge of Y aspects. Thank you very much, Luke.

www.ingramcontent.com/pod-product-compliance
Lightning Source LLC
Chambersburg PA
CBHW052121030426
42335CB00025B/3078